MW01282003

READY TO GO VEGAN?

A Guide for Making the
Transition to a Plant-Based Diet
Simple, Affordable & DAM Good!

Written by Danni McGhee

Printed in the United States of America

First Printing, 2018

ISBN 978-1729386033

Indigenous Millennials Publishing
5137 Astor Place, SE, Suite 1
Washington, DC 20019

www.DAMGoodVegan.com

This book is dedicated to you;
I wish you much success on your vegan journey.

Special Thanks

So many names to name. I appreciate you all that have supported me through my vegan journey, I love you so very much! ~ I give thanks to the individuals and companies that pre-ordered a copy of this book. Your support means the world to me. Much love to all.

~ Lauren Epps ~

~ Shon Bujack Evans ~

~ Darryl Lewis ~

~ Delmar Obaji ~

~ Tonae Holley ~
"I am proud of you and your journey. I appreciate your tenacity to launch your business and stay true to yourself."

~ Claudia Gonzalez ~
Maternal and Doula Support Services
Cookie La Doula | CookieLaDoula.com

~ Michelle J. Coker M.P.A., M.A ~
Film Production and Media Company.
Telling Stories that Open Worlds...
www.OpenVoiceMedia.com

~ The Royal Feast ~
Plant-based Meal Catering where clients will enjoy healthy savory meals prepared for them that feeds their temple (body) |
TheRoyalFeast.com

James Tate
Helping you become totally "Fat" free (Mental, Spiritual, Emotional, Physical) & improve overall health | BeyondW8Loss.com

~ Jessica Posley ~

~ Allison Frith ~

~ Tanisha Wallace ~

~ Mark Howard ~
"It is not in the stars to hold our destiny but in ourselves." W. Shakespeare

~ Cassie Jackson ~
"All life deserves respect, dignity, and compassion."

~ Jacki Rooths ~
A place of peace, the joy of total liberation within!
www.soulfullyraw.com

Ri Taylor
Dog Educator & Photographer
RedemptionDogEducation.com
facebook.com/RiTaylorStudios

~ Andy Never ~
Finding plant-based meals prepared with wholesome ingredients is easy with HomeSheff | www.HomeSheff.com

~ Sara Swetzoff ~
DC Childcare Collective
"Childcare as a form of political solidarity" | dcchildcarecollective.org

"IN THIS FOOD I SEE CLEARLY THE PRESENCE OF THE ENTIRE UNIVERSE SUPPORTING MY EXISTENCE."
– THICH NHAT HANH

AFFIRMATION FOR POSITIVE HEALTH

Flow of Contents

TODAY, I EAT FOR NOURISHMENT

AFFIRMATION FOR POSITIVE HEALTH

Introduction

Greetings & Love! My name is Danni McGhee, and I am your plant-based nutrition coach. I am so excited to be sharing this book with you! I remember when I first went vegan, I had support and guidance, which I believe was the #1 reason I was so successful in my transition.

This is book is a way to give back and pass the information that I have gathered over the years of being vegan. It is my intention that this book be more of a workbook that you journal in, jot down notes in the margin area, and take with you to the grocery store when you're stocking up on plant-based ingredients.

Most importantly, I'd love this book to serve as a support tool to not only help you get an understanding on what it meas to eat a plant-based diet, but also assist you in staying on track as you transition your diet. There is space to journal directly in this book, but we do suggest you continue to write in your own personal journal. I have also included a 30-Day Vegan Success Tracker at the end of the book so you can log your meals and water intake, track your workouts, write in affirmations for positive health, and record what you did every day to practice self-love.

We have included all of these aspects because optimal health involves taking care of mind, body, and soul. Sending you love and light on your journey. Enjoy the ride.

I'M MAKING COMPASSIONATE CHOICES FOR MYSELF

AFFIRMATION FOR POSITIVE HEALTH

What's the Difference Between Vegan & Plant-Based?

A plant-based vegan diet consists of all vegetables, fruits, grains, nuts, seeds, and legumes. It excludes consuming any meat, dairy, eggs, and any animal by-products.

A vegan lifestyle refers to more than just diet. As a vegan, compassion for animals is considered in all areas of life. Vegans would not buy leather, silk or fur, visit aquariums, circuses, and zoos, eat honey, purchase pets from pet breeders, or use products that have been tested on animals. This lifestyle is intended to honor animals as the sentient beings with feelings and not use and abuse them for human consumption.

This book is focused on the benefits of a plant-based diet and sharing tips on how to make the transition less challenging. The terms plant-based and vegan when referring to diet are interchangeable at times, but not in all cases.

Fruits, vegetables, nuts, seeds, legumes, and grains are both vegan and plant-based because they do not contain any animal products or by-products and are consumed with minimal processing. Foods likes guacamole, hummus, peanut butter, vegetable broth, applesauce, and salsa are examples of minimally processed plant-based foods.

Condiments like mustard, ketchup, and vinegar are also in the same category. Corn tortilla, though slightly more processed than the items names above, would still be considered plant-based food.

There are vegan food options that are available that would not be considered plant-based. A few examples are Oreos, Skittles, potato chips, french fries, sodas, vegan cheese, and faux meats. These foods would be considered plant-fragments because they do contain plant-based ingredients, but due to being highly processed, they do not contain the same nutritional value and health benefits as does whole plant-based foods.

These vegan food options are excellent during your transition or when you want to indulge in some junk food! But, keep in mind that these foods should be no more than 20% of your diet. The body thrives when fueled with whole, organic, plant-based food because of their high nutrition value, as well as their water and fiber content. These food options not only nourish the body, but also promote a healthy digestive system, increases detoxification, and allows the body to begin to heal and re-calibrate.

A plant-based vegan diet is the fastest way to optimal health and overall well-being. When you choose to keep a plant-based diet, you are choosing compassion. You are not contributing to the abuse and murder of animals for your own personal gain. It is possible to live without consuming animals, so by consciously making that choice, you are becoming a part of the solution.

There is an increasingly growing problem happening on our planet that most are not aware of or decide to turn a blind eye to it. As the population of the planet continue to grow, the demand for more food increases. With that increase, the factory farms are becoming more aggressive in their attempts to meet these demands. If you are more interested in learning about the common practices in the meat and dairy industry, watch the "Earthlings" and "Cowspiracy" documentaries. They are both very eye opening and contains insightful information that can help you be more aware of where your food and other consumable products come from.

By making the decision to keep a plant-based diet and lead a vegan lifestyle, you are choosing a life of compassion!

I EAT WELL SO THAT I CAN LIVE WELL

AFFIRMATION FOR POSITIVE HEALTH

Do Vegans Only Eat Salads & Smoothies?

Of course not! A plant-based diet is filled with all the same foods that everyone loves to enjoy. As an omnivore, I enjoyed eating all types of food from all cuisines. I definitely considered myself a "foodie" and enjoyed trying new things. Now that I have chosen to keep a plant-based diet, I still LOVE food, and enjoy discovering new ways to create plant-based meals.

I learned very early in my transition that I could easily veganize nearly everything that I used to eat. "Anything you can eat, I can eat vegan" was my new favorite motto. With some research, I found out what others vegans would use as replacements, then I'd head to the kitchen and put my own magic on it. Each time I recreated a new meal, I was pleasantly surprised that food could still satisfy my palate and feed my soul in a completely new way. There was a beautiful feeling that came over me knowing that no animals were harmed in the making of my choices.

I fell in love with food all over again, and reinvented my recipes. I veganized tacos, nachos, chili, burgers, lasagna, buffalo wings, curry masala, jerk chicken, fried rice, brownies, macaroni & cheese, potato salad, hot dogs, crab cakes, I mean... literally everything! So be encouraged that you will not be losing out on your favorite meals. And you may even discover some new foods that you never thought you liked.

MY BODY GETS ALL THE NUTRIENTS IT NEEDS

AFFIRMATION FOR POSITIVE HEALTH

What are the Benefits of a Plant-Based Diet?

A plant-based diet is the fastest way to optimal health. By eliminating the foods that are causing "dis-ease", the body is able to heal and release most of the ailments you may be suffering with right now. When I speak of 'dis-ease", I am referring to any ailment that is reducing our vitality. Our bodies are powerful machines that are designed to detox what is not serving us. When we consume foods that are highly acidic, like meat, dairy, eggs, and highly processed foods, our body begins to lose the fight for wellness within. Our bodies need the assistance of proper nutrition, rest, hydration, breathing, and physical activity to thrive and keep "dis-ease" at bay.

Everyone's results will be different, but the common benefit is that you will feel a shift in your physical body as well as your mental, emotional, and spiritual bodies. Going vegan and transitioning to a plant-based diet is a transformative process, and you may notice along your journey that your decision to keep a plant-based diet brings more awareness and potentially healing to your every aspect of your life.

You will probably experience some detox symptoms, but don't let that discourage you. After the initial discomfort of detoxing (fatigue, skin breakouts, etc.), within days, you will begin experiencing the positive effects.

THIS FOOD IS HEALING ME

AFFIRMATION FOR POSITIVE HEALTH

+ Weight loss

+ Fatigue (at first as your body is adjusting to your new diet)

+ Improved sleep quality

+ Increased energy

+ More frequent urination or bowel movements

+ Skin breakouts

+ Improved digestion

+ Clearer skin, longer nails, shinier hair

+ Better smelling body odor

+ Fewer menstruation symptoms

+ Less joint pain

+ Decreased feelings of anxiety & depression

+ Improved overall mood

+ Heightened awareness & intuition

+ Your tastebuds come to life

+ Better performance in physical activities

+ Increased libido

+ PLUS MORE! There are simply too many list!

Everyone will experience different symptoms, so do not compare your journey to others. Continue to document your personal journey and stay focused on your health goals.

I AM WILLING TO SLOW DOWN & TAKE THIS TIME TO NOURISH MYSELF

AFFIRMATION FOR POSITIVE HEALTH

Do I Have to Go Cold-Turkey?

Transitioning to a vegan diet is a personal journey and everyone transitions in different ways. There's no right or wrong way to your new goal of eating a vegan diet. It really comes down to what you can take on at this present moment. You have to be ready mentally for any change, so if your feeling like you're ready to go cold-turkey, do it! If you're ready to start with cutting out certain things progressively over time, then do that! Either way, you'll reach your goal.

If you're going to transition slowly by gradually eliminating animal-based products from your diet, be sure you have a plan of action to stay on course to your overall goal. Journal about your why and all the reasons you're committing to this transition, and refer back to it often.

If you're going to go cold-turkey, be prepared and get support asap. You'll want to have an idea of what recipes you want to try, the vegan pantry and fridge staples you'll need, and the time to allow for the learning curve. Going cold-turkey is absolutely possible as long as you're prepared and feel supported.

In both instances, support is necessary. It's great to have vegan friends, attend vegan events, join a vegan transition course, or get a coach to guide you along.

EVERY CELL IN MY BODY VIBRATES GOOD HEALTH

AFFIRMATION FOR POSITIVE HEALTH

What's My Why?

Changing your diet and lifestyle is a very important and transformational period in your life. If you are reading this book, it means you have considered taking the leap to a plant-based diet, so now it's time to talk about why you're making this decision. In the next few pages, you will be able to write down your thoughts and health goals. Refer back to this whenever you need encouragement or motivation to keep pressing forward if negative thoughts creep in making you may consider giving up. Staying positive and open during this transitional time is important for a success transition!

AFFIRMATIONS FOR GOOD HEALTH

+ *I am a conscious eater.*

+ *I feel energized and happy when I eat well.*

+ *Nothing tastes as good as healthy feels.*

+ *I take time to prepare healthy meals.*

+ *Eating healthy nourishes my body and soul.*

+ *I have a positive relationship with food.*

+ *I am healed, whole, and healthy.*

+ *I am thankful for what my body allows me to do.*

+ *I am focused on providing proper nutrition to my body.*

+ *My body is getting stronger and healthier every day.*

Take some time to write down your why. Why have you chosen to transition to a plant-based diet? What are the results you are looking for? What's in it for you in the end? How will you celebrate reaching this goal?

_____

_____

_____

_____

_____

_____

_____

_____

EATING RIGHT IS EASY & FUN FOR ME – I LOVE MY BODY AND TAKE GOOD CARE OF IT BY EATING CORRECTLY

AFFIRMATION FOR POSITIVE HEALTH

Should I Continue Journmaling?

Now that you have written out your why, your goals, and what's in it for you by completing these goals, it can also be beneficial to continue documenting your journey.

JOURNAL SUGGESTIONS & PROMPTS

+ Write down why you want to do this challenge.

+ Jot down your weight and body measurements to track physical changes.

+ Document how you're feeling emotionally.

+ Journal about your how your body is changing physically.

+ Describe your mental state of mind.

+ Any spiritual experiences that have come from your diet change?

Write in your journal any other feelings you're experiencing daily. There are no limits or rules to how you can journal. Just start writing out your thoughts. As you grow through your transition, you can refer back to these journal entries to see how far you have come.

The Vegan Success Journal is an awesome health tracker to document your transition. This 66-day journal will keep you motivated and allows for you to document your transition experience. Order your copy at www.VeganSuccessJournal.com!

I ALWAYS LISTEN TO MY BODY

AFFIRMATION FOR POSITIVE HEALTH

Why Is It Important for Me to Go Vegan?

We feel empowered with more knowledge. Spend an afternoon this weekend watching a documentary about how a plant-based diet can benefit your health, the animals, and the planet.

There are a few to choose from, but here are my recommendations that are available on Netflix:

+ What The Health   + Cowspiracy

+ Forks Over Knives   + Earthlings

From here, continue to seek the truth about where your food is coming from and how it impacts your health, the Earth, and other beings. There is so much research available at our fingertips, and by taking a little time to do your own research, watch documentaries, and read books about veganism and a plant-based diet, you will be armed with the knowledge to backup your why.

For more specific information, take a moment to google "plant-based diet and [inset ailment or condition you or a loved one may be dealing with.] Research animal agriculture and it's effects on our planet. You will find tons of information that can help you make the best and most informed decisions regarding your food choices.

I OPENLY GIVE & RECEIVE LOVE

AFFIRMATION FOR POSITIVE HEALTH

But I Don't Know Anyone Who's Vegan?

It can be very comforting to be around others that are on the same journey as you. Search for a vegan group or events in your area. Find local happenings by using Meetup.com, Eventbrite.com, and Facebook.com; just type in "vegan", and tons of results will pop up! You can also join online support groups on Facebook. These groups are great inspiration and motivation! You may even meet a new friend here. I've met a few friends online that are now friends in "real life". Having the support of local vegan friends was so comforting. It was nice to know I had people I could go out to eat with or that could cook for me without me worrying about the ingredients they used. Support and community is everything.

Where Do I Find Vegan Food?

FIND A LOCAL VEGAN RESTAURANT

We advocate for preparing your meals at home as much as possible, but we lead busy lives and that is not always feasible. Finding local vegan restaurants and vegan options can make your transition easier. Happy Cow and Vanilla Bean are two great apps to download to find local vegan fare. Big cities will have more options but you'll be surprised that there are new vegan restaurants popping up everywhere! Check back to those apps often to see what's new in your town.

I AM LEARNING NEW THINGS THAT HEAL MY BODY ONE STEP AT A TIME

AFFIRMATION FOR POSITIVE HEALTH

Ask for their vegan or vegetarian menu. If they offer a vegetarian menu, find options where you removing the dairy/egg products would be easy to do without modifying the dish too much. Also, skim over restaurant menu ingredients, and ask if they can make you something custom using their plant-based ingredients. For example, I love asking for sauteed veggies in marinara sauce over noodles. If all else fails, check out their sides and salads. They may have something to work with here.

If possible, research the restaurant before heading there so you know what they offer. You can also call ahead and ask the kitchen manager what they would suggest for vegan options. If they unable to accommodate you, try a different restaurant. There are some restaurants that you are guaranteed to find a vegan option: Indian, Asian, and Ethiopian are always a safe bet.

Ok, I'm Ready to Go Vegan! Now what?

Now that you're ready to transition to a plant-based diet or vegan lifestyle, find resources that will help you be successful on your journey. Join local and online groups that will keep you inspired and motivated to reach your health goals. Watch documentaries and read as many books as you can about plant-based food and a vegan lifestyle. Be open to trying new things and keep a positive mindset throughout the process.

I AM WORTH THE TIME & MONEY I INVEST IN MY HEALTH

AFFIRMATION FOR POSITIVE HEALTH

DAM Good Vegan offers comprehensive online courses that will walk you through all aspects of a plant-based diet and assist you with transitioning by supporting you with self-guided course material, weekly group coaching webinars, discussion forums, and other support tools. We'll hold your hand, so you can successfully thrive on a plant-based diet. We're passionate about making the transition to a plant-based diet simple, affordable, and DAM Good!

Sometimes, we need more personalized and one-on one assistance on our journey. We also understand that this information can be overwhelming. There is so much to learn about a plant-based diet it can be discouraging when you don't know exactly what you're looking for within your research.

Our Ready to Go Vegan Online Course has a comprehensive curriculum covering all aspects of a plant-based diet. We cover everything from the benefits, detox symptoms, typical vegan meals, where you'll get your nutrients, and veganizing your kitchen PLUS a 7-day meal plan, access to our recipes site, grocery lists, and weekly live Q&A calls for group coaching. Enroll in our Ready to Go Vegan Online Course at www.ReadyToGoVegan.com.

If you'd like more personalized coaching, you can book a strategy sessions with me so we can get you on track and keep you motivated. Book a strategy session at www.VeganStrategySession.com.

PLANNING HEALTHY MEALS IS A JOY

AFFIRMATION FOR POSITIVE HEALTH

FIND DAM GOOD VEGAN RECIPES

Find the recipes to all meal suggestions in the 7-Day Meal Plan at www.TheVeganSkillet.com. Create a login and you'll see all of these recipes included in the free trial. Become a member to gain access to hundreds of plant-based vegan recipes!

If you become a member of our recipe site, you'll receive a new 7-Day Meal Plan every month plus gain access to grocery lists, meal prep and on-the-go tips, and a video library with cooking demos. It is our intention for this resource to give you the confidence to prepare amazing vegan meals in your own kitchen.

READY TO GO VEGAN

7-DAY MEAL PLAN

THIS MEAL PLAN OFFERS SUGGESTIONS FOR ALL YOUR MEALS PLUS SNACKS, DESSERTS, & BEVERAGES FOR 7 DAYS!

MONDAY

DAY 1

Yummy Green Smoothie
BREAKFAST

Tasty Grilled Cheese
LUNCH

Pineapple Fried RIce
DINNER

TUESDAY

DAY 2

Really Good Oatmeal
BREAKFAST

Super Green Boost Salad
LUNCH

Vegan Crab Cakes
DINNER

WEDNESDAY

DAY 3

Yummy Green Smoothie
BREAKFAST

Raw Vegan Tacos
LUNCH

Curry Chickpea Stew
DINNER

THURSDAY

DAY 4

Super Bomb Chia Pudding
BREAKFAST

Super Green Boost Salad
LUNCH

Spinach Alfredo Pasta
DINNER

FRIDAY

DAY 5

Yummy Green Smoothie
BREAKFAST

Buffalo Chickpea Nuggets
LUNCH

Mediterranean Falafel Pita Wrap
DINNER

Find these recipes at www.TheVeganSkillet.com

GET THESE RECIPES

FIND THESE RECIPES AT THEVEGANSKILLET.COM.

SIMPLY CREATE AN ACCOUNT TO ACCESS 30+ DELICIOUS VEGAN RECIPES!

BECOME A MEMBER FOR FULL ACCESS TO HUNDREDS OF RECIPES & MEAL PREP TIPS & SUPPORT.

SATURDAY

DAY 6

Mango Avocado Toast
BREAKFAST

BBQ Jackfruit Tacos
LUNCH

Chili & Cornbread
DINNER

SUNDAY

DAY 7

Veggie & Sausage Grits Bowl
BREAKFAST

Vegan Tuna Melts
LUNCH

Baked Ziti & Garlic Bread
DINNER

SNACKS

MUNCH

Guacamole
SNACK #1

Date Balls
SNACK #2

Grab Dip
SNACK #3

BEVERAGES

SIP

Hot Chocolate
BEVERAGE #1

Cashew Milk
BEVERAGE #2

Chai Tea Latte
BEVERAGE #3

DESSERTS

INDULGE

Strawberry Shake
DESSERT #1

Rice Krispy Treats
DESSERT #2

Brownies
DESSERT #3

HELLO, KITCHEN, YOU ARE MY NOURISHMENT CENTER – I APPRECIATE YOU!

AFFIRMATION FOR POSITIVE HEALTH

Veganize Your Kitchen

Veganize your kitchen with these 3 simple steps:

Step 1 Go through everything in your pantry and fridge. Throw away anything that has expired. Donate non-vegan foods that are still good. Restock your fridge and pantry with all the vegan/plant-based ingredients that you're left with. Your fridge and pantry may be looking a bare after this step, but now this gives you opportunity to fill your kitchen with all the ingredients you'll need to create plant-based meals. So let's go shopping!

Step 2 Refer to the *Vegan Grocery List* on page 35 as you are in the grocery store. By keeping your kitchen stocked with these vegan staples, you will always have on hand what you need.

Step 3 Take inventory of your kitchen tools and compare to our Kitchen Essentials list on page 37. Having the right tools to create your meals will make meal prep much more efficient and fun.

That's it! Your kitchen is officially veganized!

I AM SO GRATEFUL TO BE CHOOSING FOOD THAT SUPPORTS MY BEST HEALTH

AFFIRMATION FOR POSITIVE HEALTH

Vegan Grocery List

FRUITS
+ Bananas
+ Berries
+ Apples
+ *choose a variety of fruit you love*

VEGETABLES
+ Spinach
+ Kale
+ Romaine
+ Potatoes
+ Onion
+ *choose a variety of veggies you love*

NUTS
+ Almonds
+ Cashews
+ Walnuts
+ Brazil Nuts

VEGAN DAIRY
+ Vegan Butter
+ Vegan Mayo
+ Vegan Cheese
+ Plant-Based Milk
+ Vegan Yogurt

OTHER
+ Vegetable Broth
+ Granola
+ Whole Grain Bread

DRIED F
+ Dates
+ Cranberries
+ Raisins
+ Mango
+ Coconut

GRAINS
+ Brown Rice
+ Oats
+ Grits
+ Popcorn
+ Pasta (*preferably gluten free*)

LEGUMES
+ Chickpeas
+ Black Beans
+ Kidney Beans
+ Lentils (All Colors)
+ Split Peas

CANNNED
+ Coconut Milk
+ Beans & Legumes
+ Diced & Crushed Tomatoes
+ Hearts of Palm

FROZEN / COLD
+ Fruit (for smoothies)
+ Mixed Veggies (for quick stir fry)
+ Beefless Crumbles
+ Vegan Burgers & Sausages
+ Jackfruit

I CAN EASILY MAKE A NUTRITIOUS, DELICIOUS MEAL

AFFIRMATION FOR POSITIVE HEALTH

Vegan Grocery List

SPICES

+ Pink Salt

+ Black Pepper

+ Garlic Powder

+ Fresh Garlic

+ Onion Powder

+ Turmeric

+ Cumin

+ Paprika

+ Curry Powder

+ Chili Powder

+ Cayenne

SEEDS

+ Quinoa

+ Wild Rice

+ Chia Seeds

+ Flaxseeds

+ Pumpkin Seeds

+ Sunflower Seeds

SWEETNERS

+ Maple Syrup

+ Coconut Sugar

+ Date Sugar

Kitchen Essentials

+ Sharp Knife

+ Wooden Cutting Board

+ High Speed Blender

+ Large Bowls (for preparation)

+ Glass Jars or Bottles (for juices)

+ Glass Containers (for leftovers)

+ Masticating Juicer

+ Food Processor

+ Dehydrator

+ Thermal Container

+ Cooler Lunch Bag

Visit the *Kitchen Essentials* tab DAMGoodVegan.com for product details.

VEGAN SUCCESS TRACKER

30-DAY HEALTH TRACKER TO SUPPORT YOUR JOURNEY TO IMPROVING YOUR HEALTH AND OVERALL WELL-BEING

I LOVE & RESPECT MY BODY

AFFIRMATION FOR POSITIVE HEALTH

USING THE VEGAN SUCCESS TRACKER

The Vegan Success Tracker is a tool to support your journey to improved health and overall well-being. By keeping a journal and record of what you have been consuming (food, water, exercise, and mindfulness), you're more likely to stay on track. The added benefit is that you're able to look back at your progress and journal entries for more motivation.

This 30-day tracker has space for you to document your food, hydration, and exercise daily. Each day, we encourage you write down an affirmation for positive health, as well as, participate in one self-love activity. Reading a book, working on your favorite craft project, taking a bath, taking yourself to the movies, or anything that you truly enjoy doing are all expressions of self-love. Find the joy in loving yourself by nourishing your mind, body, and soul.

There will also be spaces to journal as you're progressing through. We encourage you to continue writing in your own personal journal.

Earlier in the book, you wrote down the reasons why you're choosing a plant-based diet, what's in it for you in the end, and how you'll celebrate reaching your goals. Refer back to this section often to remind yourself of the commitment you have made to yourself. Remember, take this one day at a time; there's no rush. Use each day to learn something and apply it the next day. You got this!

JOURNAL:BEFORE

Write down anything you're feeling or noticing as you prepare to begin eating a plant-based diet. You can record your weight, body measurements, or any ailments you're experiencing in this moment. Think about where you are mentally, emotionally, and spiritually. Document those thoughts. Write down what you are grateful for and how you plan to stay motivated.

_____

_____

_____

_____

_____

_____

_____

_____ *[continue writing in our personal journal]*

EVERY DAY IS A NEW DAY FILLED WITH JOY & HEALTH

AFFIRMATION FOR POSITIVE HEALTH

HEALTH TRACKER

FOOD | WATER | EXERCISE | MINDFULNESS

DATE _____/_____/_____

BREAKFAST

LUNCH

DINNER

SNACK/DESSERT

AFFIRMATION
FOR POSITIVE HEALTH

SELF LOVE ACTIVITY
SOMETHING FOR YOU

EXERCISE
DID YOU WORKOUT?

HYDRATION
EACH GLASS = 16 OZ

I AM A CONSCIOUS EATER

AFFIRMATION FOR POSITIVE HEALTH

HEALTH TRACKER

F O O D | W A T E R | E X E R C I S E | M I N D F U L N E S S

DATE _____/_____/_____

BREAKFAST

LUNCH

DINNER

SNACK/DESSERT

AFFIRMATION
FOR POSITIVE HEALTH

SELF LOVE ACTIVITY
SOMETHING FOR YOU

EXERCISE
DID YOU WORKOUT?

HYDRATION
EACH GLASS = 16 OZ

I CHOOSE HEALTH AND WELLNESS OVER RESTRICTIVE DIETS

AFFIRMATION FOR POSITIVE HEALTH

HEALTH TRACKER

FOOD | WATER | EXERCISE | MINDFULNESS

DATE _____/_____/_____

BREAKFAST

LUNCH

DINNER

SNACK/DESSERT

AFFIRMATION
FOR POSITIVE HEALTH

SELF LOVE ACTIVITY
SOMETHING FOR YOU

EXERCISE
DID YOU WORKOUT?

HYDRATION
EACH GLASS = 16 OZ

I JOYFULLY OBSERVE THE TASTES & TEXTURES OF THIS FOOD

AFFIRMATION FOR POSITIVE HEALTH

HEALTH TRACKER

FOOD | WATER | EXERCISE | MINDFULNESS

DATE _____/_____/_____

BREAKFAST

LUNCH

DINNER

SNACK/DESSERT

AFFIRMATION
FOR POSITIVE HEALTH

SELF LOVE ACTIVITY
SOMETHING FOR YOU

EXERCISE
DID YOU WORKOUT?

HYDRATION
EACH GLASS = 16 OZ

I FEEL ENERGIZED & HAPPY WHEN I EAT WELL

AFFIRMATION FOR POSITIVE HEALTH

HEALTH TRACKER

FOOD | WATER | EXERCISE | MINDFULNESS

DATE _____/_____/_____

BREAKFAST

LUNCH

DINNER

SNACK/DESSERT

AFFIRMATION
FOR POSITIVE HEALTH

SELF LOVE ACTIVITY
SOMETHING FOR YOU

EXERCISE
DID YOU WORKOUT?

HYDRATION
EACH GLASS = 16 OZ

I RELEASE PAST GUILT & NEGATIVE FEELINGS ABOUT EATING

AFFIRMATION FOR POSITIVE HEALTH

HEALTH TRACKER

FOOD | WATER | EXERCISE | MINDFULNESS

DATE _____/_____/_____

BREAKFAST

LUNCH

DINNER

SNACK/DESSERT

AFFIRMATION
FOR POSITIVE HEALTH

SELF LOVE ACTIVITY
SOMETHING FOR YOU

EXERCISE
DID YOU WORKOUT?

HYDRATION
EACH GLASS = 16 OZ

I DO A HEALTHY AMOUNT OF EXERCISE REGULARLY

AFFIRMATION FOR POSITIVE HEALTH

HEALTH TRACKER

FOOD | WATER | EXERCISE | MINDFULNESS

DATE _____/_____/_____

BREAKFAST

LUNCH

DINNER

SNACK/DESSERT

AFFIRMATION
FOR POSITIVE HEALTH

SELF LOVE ACTIVITY
SOMETHING FOR YOU

EXERCISE
DID YOU WORKOUT?

HYDRATION
EACH GLASS = 16 OZ

I HAVE EVERYTHING I NEED TO HELP ME PREPARE DELICIOUS, NUTRITIOUS MEALS

AFFIRMATION FOR POSITIVE HEALTH

HEALTH TRACKER

FOOD | WATER | EXERCISE | MINDFULNESS

||||||||||||||||||||||||||||||||||||||||||||||||||||||||||||||||||||||||||||||||||||||||||||

DATE _____/_____/_____

BREAKFAST

LUNCH

DINNER

SNACK/DESSERT

AFFIRMATION
FOR POSITIVE HEALTH

SELF LOVE ACTIVITY
SOMETHING FOR YOU

EXERCISE
DID YOU WORKOUT?

HYDRATION
EACH GLASS = 16 OZ

I FEEL GOOD ABOUT MYSELF

AFFIRMATION FOR POSITIVE HEALTH

HEALTH TRACKER

FOOD | WATER | EXERCISE | MINDFULNESS

DATE _____/_____/_____

BREAKFAST

LUNCH

DINNER

SNACK/DESSERT

AFFIRMATION
FOR POSITIVE HEALTH

SELF LOVE ACTIVITY
SOMETHING FOR YOU

EXERCISE
DID YOU WORKOUT?

HYDRATION
EACH GLASS = 16 OZ

MY BODY HEALS & STRENGTHENS WITH EVERY BITE I TAKE

AFFIRMATION FOR POSITIVE HEALTH

HEALTH TRACKER

FOOD | WATER | EXERCISE | MINDFULNESS

|||||||||||||||||||||||||||||||||||||||||||||||||||||||||||||||||||||||||||||||||||||||||||

DATE _____/_____/_____

BREAKFAST

LUNCH

DINNER

SNACK/DESSERT

AFFIRMATION
FOR POSITIVE HEALTH

SELF LOVE ACTIVITY
SOMETHING FOR YOU

EXERCISE
DID YOU WORKOUT?

HYDRATION
EACH GLASS = 16 OZ

I'M ALLOWING MY BODY TO GUIDE MY FOOD AWARENESS

Yay! It's been 10 days, and you're still here! Are you noticing any changes both positive or negative? What have you learned that has been a game changer so far? What will you focus on for the next few days?

_____

_____

_____

_____

_____

_____

_____

_____ [continue writing in our personal journal]

I MAKE POWERFUL CHOICES ABOUT FOOD

AFFIRMATION FOR POSITIVE HEALTH

HEALTH TRACKER

FOOD | WATER | EXERCISE | MINDFULNESS

|||||||||||||||||||||||||||||||||||||||||||||||||||||||||||||||||||||||||||||||||||||||||||||

DATE _____/_____/_____

BREAKFAST

LUNCH

DINNER

SNACK/DESSERT

AFFIRMATION
FOR POSITIVE HEALTH

SELF LOVE ACTIVITY
SOMETHING FOR YOU

EXERCISE
DID YOU WORKOUT?

HYDRATION
EACH GLASS = 16 OZ

I FORGIVE MYSELF FOR EATING THE WRONG FOODS & I TRANSCEND ALL FEELINGS OF UNWORTHINESS

AFFIRMATION FOR POSITIVE HEALTH

HEALTH TRACKER

FOOD | WATER | EXERCISE | MINDFULNESS

DATE _____/_____/_____

BREAKFAST

LUNCH

DINNER

SNACK/DESSERT

AFFIRMATION
FOR POSITIVE HEALTH

SELF LOVE ACTIVITY
SOMETHING FOR YOU

EXERCISE
DID YOU WORKOUT?

HYDRATION
EACH GLASS = 16 OZ

I LOVE SPENDING TIME IN THE KITCHEN

AFFIRMATION FOR POSITIVE HEALTH

HEALTH TRACKER

FOOD | WATER | EXERCISE | MINDFULNESS

DATE _____/_____/_____

BREAKFAST

LUNCH

DINNER

SNACK/DESSERT

AFFIRMATION
FOR POSITIVE HEALTH

SELF LOVE ACTIVITY
SOMETHING FOR YOU

EXERCISE
DID YOU WORKOUT?

HYDRATION
EACH GLASS = 16 OZ

MY FAMILY LOVES TO EAT HEALTHY FOOD

AFFIRMATION FOR POSITIVE HEALTH

HEALTH TRACKER

FOOD | WATER | EXERCISE | MINDFULNESS

DATE _____/_____/_____

BREAKFAST

LUNCH

DINNER

SNACK/DESSERT

AFFIRMATION
FOR POSITIVE HEALTH

SELF LOVE ACTIVITY
SOMETHING FOR YOU

EXERCISE
DID YOU WORKOUT?

HYDRATION
EACH GLASS = 16 OZ

73

I AM WELL NOURISHED IN PREPARATION FOR THE DAY AHEAD OF ME

AFFIRMATION FOR POSITIVE HEALTH

HEALTH TRACKER

FOOD | WATER | EXERCISE | MINDFULNESS

DATE _____/_____/_____

BREAKFAST

LUNCH

DINNER

SNACK/DESSERT

AFFIRMATION
FOR POSITIVE HEALTH

SELF LOVE ACTIVITY
SOMETHING FOR YOU

EXERCISE
DID YOU WORKOUT?

HYDRATION
EACH GLASS = 16 OZ

I AM THANKFUL FOR WHAT MY BODY ALLOWS ME TO DO

AFFIRMATION FOR POSITIVE HEALTH

HEALTH TRACKER

FOOD | WATER | EXERCISE | MINDFULNESS

||||||||||||||||||||||||||||||||||||||||||||||||||||||||||||||||||||||||||||||||||||||||

DATE _____/_____/_____

BREAKFAST

LUNCH

DINNER

SNACK/DESSERT

AFFIRMATION
FOR POSITIVE HEALTH

SELF LOVE ACTIVITY
SOMETHING FOR YOU

EXERCISE
DID YOU WORKOUT?

HYDRATION
EACH GLASS = 16 OZ

I AM FOCUSED ON PROVIDING PROPER NUTRITION TO MY BODY

AFFIRMATION FOR POSITIVE HEALTH

HEALTH TRACKER

FOOD | WATER | EXERCISE | MINDFULNESS

DATE _____/_____/_____

BREAKFAST

LUNCH

DINNER

SNACK/DESSERT

AFFIRMATION
FOR POSITIVE HEALTH

SELF LOVE ACTIVITY
SOMETHING FOR YOU

EXERCISE
DID YOU WORKOUT?

HYDRATION
EACH GLASS = 16 OZ

WITH EACH BITE, I FEEL MORE ENERGIZED

AFFIRMATION FOR POSITIVE HEALTH

HEALTH TRACKER

FOOD | WATER | EXERCISE | MINDFULNESS

|||||||||||||||||||||||||||||||||||||||||||||||||||||||||||||||||||||||||||||||||||||||||||

DATE _____ / _____ / _____

BREAKFAST

LUNCH

DINNER

SNACK/DESSERT

AFFIRMATION
FOR POSITIVE HEALTH

SELF LOVE ACTIVITY
SOMETHING FOR YOU

EXERCISE
DID YOU WORKOUT?

HYDRATION
EACH GLASS = 16 OZ

I LISTEN FOR WHEN I AM SATISFIED & FULL

AFFIRMATION FOR POSITIVE HEALTH

HEALTH TRACKER

F O O D | W A T E R | E X E R C I S E | M I N D F U L N E S S

DATE _____/_____/_____

BREAKFAST

LUNCH

DINNER

SNACK/DESSERT

AFFIRMATION
FOR POSITIVE HEALTH

SELF LOVE ACTIVITY
SOMETHING FOR YOU

EXERCISE
DID YOU WORKOUT?

HYDRATION
EACH GLASS = 16 OZ

I AM HEALED, WHOLE, & HEALTHY

AFFIRMATION FOR POSITIVE HEALTH

HEALTH TRACKER

FOOD | WATER | EXERCISE | MINDFULNESS

DATE _____/_____/_____

BREAKFAST

LUNCH

DINNER

SNACK/DESSERT

AFFIRMATION
FOR POSITIVE HEALTH

SELF LOVE ACTIVITY
SOMETHING FOR YOU

EXERCISE
DID YOU WORKOUT?

HYDRATION
EACH GLASS = 16 OZ

NOTHING TASTES AS GOOD AS HEALTHY FEELS

AFFIRMATION FOR POSITIVE HEALTH

Well, look at you, Superstar! Tomorrow you'll have been following along this success tracker for 3 weeks! You're well on your way now! How are you feeling physically, mentally, emotionally, and spiritually? How has your body been responding to a plant-based diet? What's been your favorite plant-based meal to eat so far? Have you attended any vegan events yet?

_____

_____

_____

_____

_____

_____

_____

_____ [continue writing in our personal journal]

I HAVE A POSITIVE RELATIONSHIP WITH FOOD

AFFIRMATION FOR POSITIVE HEALTH

HEALTH TRACKER

FOOD | WATER | EXERCISE | MINDFULNESS

DATE _____/_____/_____

BREAKFAST

LUNCH

DINNER

SNACK/DESSERT

AFFIRMATION
FOR POSITIVE HEALTH

SELF LOVE ACTIVITY
SOMETHING FOR YOU

EXERCISE
DID YOU WORKOUT?

HYDRATION
EACH GLASS = 16 OZ

THIS FOOD IS THE FOUNDATION FOR MY HEALTHY LIFESTYLE

AFFIRMATION FOR POSITIVE HEALTH

HEALTH TRACKER

FOOD | WATER | EXERCISE | MINDFULNESS

DATE _____/_____/_____

BREAKFAST

LUNCH

DINNER

SNACK/DESSERT

AFFIRMATION
FOR POSITIVE HEALTH

SELF LOVE ACTIVITY
SOMETHING FOR YOU

EXERCISE
DID YOU WORKOUT?

HYDRATION
EACH GLASS = 16 OZ

I'M FREE FROM OLD NEGATIVE PATTERNS & HABITS THAT INVOLVED FOOD

AFFIRMATION FOR POSITIVE HEALTH

HEALTH TRACKER

FOOD | WATER | EXERCISE | MINDFULNESS

DATE _____/_____/_____

BREAKFAST

LUNCH

DINNER

SNACK/DESSERT

AFFIRMATION
FOR POSITIVE HEALTH

SELF LOVE ACTIVITY
SOMETHING FOR YOU

EXERCISE
DID YOU WORKOUT?

HYDRATION
EACH GLASS = 16 OZ

ALL THAT I NEED IS WITHIN ME

AFFIRMATION FOR POSITIVE HEALTH

HEALTH TRACKER

FOOD | WATER | EXERCISE | MINDFULNESS

||||||||||||||||||||||||||||||||||||||||||||||||||||||||||||||||||||||||||||||||||||||||||||||||||||||||||

DATE _____/_____/_____

BREAKFAST

LUNCH

DINNER

SNACK/DESSERT

AFFIRMATION
FOR POSITIVE HEALTH

SELF LOVE ACTIVITY
SOMETHING FOR YOU

EXERCISE
DID YOU WORKOUT?

HYDRATION
EACH GLASS = 16 OZ

MY TASTE BUDS ARE CHANGING EVERY DAY– I NO LONGER CRAVE FOODS THAT DON'T NOURISH ME

AFFIRMATION FOR POSITIVE HEALTH

HEALTH TRACKER

FOOD | WATER | EXERCISE | MINDFULNESS

DATE _____/_____/_____

BREAKFAST

LUNCH

DINNER

SNACK/DESSERT

AFFIRMATION
FOR POSITIVE HEALTH

SELF LOVE ACTIVITY
SOMETHING FOR YOU

EXERCISE
DID YOU WORKOUT?

HYDRATION
EACH GLASS = 16 OZ

MY BODY IS GETTING STRONGER & HEALTHIER EVERY DAY

AFFIRMATION FOR POSITIVE HEALTH

HEALTH TRACKER

FOOD | WATER | EXERCISE | MINDFULNESS

||||||||||||||||||||||||||||||||||||||||||||||||||||||||||||||||||||||||||||||||||||||||||||||||||||

DATE _____/_____/_____

BREAKFAST

LUNCH

DINNER

SNACK/DESSERT

AFFIRMATION
FOR POSITIVE HEALTH

SELF LOVE ACTIVITY
SOMETHING FOR YOU

EXERCISE
DID YOU WORKOUT?

HYDRATION
EACH GLASS = 16 OZ

I TAKE TIME TO PREPARE HEALTHY MEALS

AFFIRMATION FOR POSITIVE HEALTH

HEALTH TRACKER

FOOD | WATER | EXERCISE | MINDFULNESS

DATE _____/_____/_____

BREAKFAST

LUNCH

DINNER

SNACK/DESSERT

AFFIRMATION
FOR POSITIVE HEALTH

SELF LOVE ACTIVITY
SOMETHING FOR YOU

EXERCISE
DID YOU WORKOUT?

HYDRATION
EACH GLASS = 16 OZ

I EAT ONLY WHEN I AM ACTUALLY HUNGRY

AFFIRMATION FOR POSITIVE HEALTH

HEALTH TRACKER

FOOD | WATER | EXERCISE | MINDFULNESS

|||||||||||||||||||||||||||||||||||||||||||||||||||||||||||||||||||||||||||||||||||||||

DATE _____/_____/_____

BREAKFAST

LUNCH

DINNER

SNACK/DESSERT

AFFIRMATION
FOR POSITIVE HEALTH

SELF LOVE ACTIVITY
SOMETHING FOR YOU

EXERCISE
DID YOU WORKOUT?

HYDRATION
EACH GLASS = 16 OZ

I FEEL GREAT WHEN I TAKE CARE OF MYSELF

AFFIRMATION FOR POSITIVE HEALTH

HEALTH TRACKER

FOOD | WATER | EXERCISE | MINDFULNESS

DATE _____/_____/_____

BREAKFAST

LUNCH

DINNER

SNACK/DESSERT

AFFIRMATION
FOR POSITIVE HEALTH

SELF LOVE ACTIVITY
SOMETHING FOR YOU

EXERCISE
DID YOU WORKOUT?

HYDRATION
EACH GLASS = 16 OZ

I AM STRONG & HEALTHY

AFFIRMATION FOR POSITIVE HEALTH

HEALTH TRACKER

FOOD | WATER | EXERCISE | MINDFULNESS

|||||||||||||||||||||||||||||||||||||||||||||||||||||||||||||||||||||||||||||||||||||||||||

DATE _____/_____/_____

BREAKFAST

LUNCH

DINNER

SNACK/DESSERT

AFFIRMATION
FOR POSITIVE HEALTH

SELF LOVE ACTIVITY
SOMETHING FOR YOU

EXERCISE
DID YOU WORKOUT?

HYDRATION
EACH GLASS = 16 OZ

EATING HEALTHY NOURISHES MY BODY AND SOUL

AFFIRMATION FOR POSITIVE HEALTH

Congratulations! You've come to day 30, and I am so proud of you! How has this experience been for you? What are the most interesting things you've learned during these 30 days? What results have you had since you've started this journey? Will you continue eating a plant-based diet on a daily basis?

_____

_____

_____

_____

_____

_____

_____

_____ [continue writing in our personal journal]

+DAM GOOD VEGAN+

We're passionate about making the transition to a plant-based diet simple,

affordable, and DAM Good! Visit our website for more company info.

www.DAMGoodVegan.com

-

+PLANT-BASED VEGAN RECIPES+

Online membership site with access to plant-based recipes, grocery lists, 7-day

meal plans, cooking demo video library, and meal prep and on-the-go tips!

www.TheVeganSkillet.com

-

+READY TO GO VEGAN ONLINE COURSES+

Online self-guided courses with a comprehensive curriculum and group

coaching to support your transition to a plant-based diet.

www.ReadyToGoVegan.com

-

+PERSONAL COACHING+

Schedule a strategy session with our Plant-Based Nutrition Coach for a

customized game plan catered to your individual needs and lifestyle.

www.VeganStrategySession.com

-

+GO VEGAN IN A WEEKEND+

If you're vegan-curious, download this free guide and experience a

weekend of plant-based eating. Take the Challenge!

www.GoVeganInAWeekend.com